# BRACE FOR THE IMPACT

A collection of poetry written by Steven Adam Simon 1981-1986

Dedicated to Terry Anne

Layout by Robert Arroyo

Edited by Judith, Terry and Tanta Flame

* Front cover photography by Jeff O'brien

Back cover photography by Steven Adam Simon

Published by Monkey Man Press, 3895 Fredonia Drive, Los Angeles CA 90068

(213) 876-2299

Manufactured in U.S.A. First printing Dec. 1986 Copyright © 1986 Steven Adam Simon ✲

ISBN 0-9605594-2-6

Printed by Augustus Art (213) 837-7151

white lace steam dreams

steep stairs come with offers of comfort

comic relief in every situation

optimists enjoy their outlook

each day brings different ways

to brace for the impact

spider spins a web dangling between branches
ants march in formation
scouting a path across windswept fields
wolves howl at an unforgiving moon
hovering beyond man's reach

lines on her cheek show slowly bleeding promises
blue webs that never grew into truth

sticky questions won't let go

compromise is diet margarine
similar texture but far from real
nature holds many ironic flavors
just when you get used to a taste
ZAP! it's time to test another recipe

playing scientist and laboratory rat grows cancerous
the only way to learn, is to watch it eat me away

— —

medicineman chants healing remedies
sickness cast away
testing lizardskin durability

lost angels choreograph a sensuous start
sunday morning calls for bermudashorts
and religious obedience

family picnics barbecue american tradition
cooking recipes that fill cozy needs

short sentence facade maintained

easy project providing clues

fresh-frozen appetizers wave around the room

heavy chomping amidst flowery conversations

see through garbage cans

delicate balance constantly achieved

worcestershire smiles help others enjoy their lives

having a child is a multi-year contract
mandatory renewal clause built in
pride of parenthood balanced by restrictive responsibility
mature is defined as ripe, fully developed

lost at sea
barely a breeze to massage full sails
whitecaps and adulthood swell across the brow
drifting with tight currents,
afraid of sighting land
salty dreams through summer,
tender schemes in hand

——

Tires sing cobblestone songs.

Rainwashed horizons cleanse perpetual impurity.

Gestures for the glance of her eye

held shut against primal pleasure.

Consumed by a unified essence.

Smudged satisfaction.

Distant tires sing cobblestone songs.

.

— —

Immense national pride
freedom clutched tightly.
Shy spectator,
watching others learn about themselves.
Thrilled to listen, scared for the world,
hoping this game doesn't get out of hand.
Pictures of Saturn,
bombs with the power of the sun.
Self-exploration exposes impressions.
Smiles are the easiest language to understand.

bad habits    early morning awakening

acceptance requested    obligation refused

purgatory    boiled in perpetual sin.

forgiveness

heaven hit quota months ago

apply for refugee status

everyone's trying desperately to get in

he'd pushed too many of the right buttons,

officially had his rank in the social order lowered:

a new level of intellectual and monetary deprivation.

The transference, although grim, went quickly.

"Adjusting is easy...." the tape repeated continually.

That's all he wanted—

for things to be easy.

CONTROL

ideas fortify ego

wild plants soak sun without image or concept

I THINK I THINK TOO MUCH

intellectualizing emotions to rescue and protect

life dares us: look beyond the surface

see how we're blinded by how we see

——

pendulum ticks faster

as we dance through blended dreamstates.

continual beginnings texture time,

encasing scattered defenses.

full commodities entail heavy responsibility.

stability forms a smoother ride in the fast lane.

cruisin'—

nice,

    smooth

        cruisin'

fantasy of some golden princess, polished far beyond reach
aluminum tongue with a silverstone finish
delivers a diamond covered speech

discarded newspapers     snowpeas vinaigrette
explosions every instant

chivalry went out with the Renaissance
no dragons left to slay
crumpled kleenex doesn't listen
just soaks in what you say

—

lavender style     midnight smile

warm eyes     soft sighs

four-four rhythm     fleeting heartbeat

endless appetite     kids in the back seat

sheep graze triumphantly     no thoughts but growing older

dusty shine     not Calvinklein

the style is permanent press

finely knitted in a polished pattern

certainly easy to bless

Pleated lines in a see-through blouse
shrunk from previous activity
Sympathetic monkey
staring at helpless lobsters crawling about
Foolish time for rhyming, taking it in stride
big city prisoner, voice echoing inside
Something not accepted, another chance to prove
getting more excited about an up and coming move

— —

Sell the kids for clubhouse seats at future races.

Collect, don't invest.

Who wants to pay for braces?

Brainwashed honesty,

authentically chilled and fresh.

Bright yellow auras,

surgically removed.

Clean atmosphere easily settles against the hills.

hidden revelations
tiger spots
bastilla
magic tricks
blended with cucumber dill

trade winds blow turquoise streamers
steel drums keep tight rhythm
pounding tribute to laughter-enhanced energy
village spirits ignite 'til dawn
celebrating breezes blow peace and purity

— —

sitting on the beach playing decoy for navy planes

this city's a prime target

eight million backbones ready to crush

Increase our defense budget

let's find more ways to kill

Our governments getting stronger

and we're footing the bill

— —

no greater desperation than

blowing your nose into a wet, used kleenex

except perhaps

putting on the same pair of filthy socks four days in a row

but such are joys one should learn to savor

sort of like smiling at kissing couples

as you fondle a blank, yet caring, page

— —

early pubescent glances
    eyes fill with classic wonder
ponder discipline possibilities
    weeds overtake gardens of innocence
explanations only put oil on the fire
religion advances into government
neither seems committed to calm
traffic signals help you avoid getting hit
one still has to look both ways

commitment is a full sense of being there

here, now, onward, forever

at moments clouds block complete sunshine

patience clears crystal views

blending our tastes creates a wide variety of spices

all flavors bring warm spine tingles

the point just arrives and sits behind them, quiet,

patiently waiting to be noticed.

basic desire shields facts from evidence.

open eyes     staring ahead

set naked     by exposed wires

whispering     hidden truths

delicate discovery

blame first molecules
one explosion after another
emerging from a common womb
problems grow to wilt in the sun
strength fertilizes tall dreams
scheming on scheduled arrivals
responses derive pleasure from being unexpected

appear ready for the next step
illusion takes concentrated energy

escapist

stereo typical showdown

double-burger society gobbles vinyl dreams

dirty countertop refuses to wipe clean

years of smoke-enforced coffeestains

thick sticky fame smeared across the wall

chips flake off previous layers

separating faded white memories

"bigger ain't da better, too cumbersome"
she speaks in lizard tongues
lashing out in all directions
no defense need be offered to her rage
yet this room feels small and sweaty
each day brings cozy readjustment
settling into a deeper trap

settling into a deeper trap
each day brings cozy readjustment
yet this room feels small and sweaty
no defense need be offered to her rage
lashing out in all directions
she speaks in lizard tongues
"bigger ain't da better, too cumbersome"

— —

mid afternoon naps require thought abandonment

cleaning musty self-shelves

throwing out parts that invite continued dust

massive thought-cleanse lightens many loads

organizing which extra tools to carry

instinct is no longer based on hunger

today, sharing comfort and creativity is my will to survive

— —

Pigeons startled into rapid flight.

Another monument towers proud over a merging crowd.

Salvation Army widows march to a volunteer beat,

fast moving across grey-black skyscape.

Diesel fumes, mounted horses in traffic,

crowded fields attract great odds.

It's getting harder to pick a winner;

rewards multiply daily in ratio with risk factors.

— —

space becomes thin as telephone line.

time-tangled vibrations

hum a quiet frenzy deep inside.

force-fed satisfaction, scrambled with thick creamy butter.

belief lies toasted and crunchy,

anxiously anticipating digestion.

crystal clear motivations bring bright reflection,

laying life thin as telephone line.

tryingtoexplaintosix-yearoldJohnnythat
Americahasaresponsibilitytotheworld
that'swhywe'respendingover300billion
dollarsayeartomaintainanarmedforce
thatprotects
            peace

pinholes in darkness

slivers of silver drip into pitchers of gold

    God's asleep

system analysis operates full function

    steel and glass enclosures dissolve moonlight

Man's expansion leaves fewer places to hide

    less silence to buffer the roar

shrinking universe

compared to limitless space

                inside

                 our

                    minds

— —

guava dreams melt a sparse ground cover

revealing bare hills of immaturity

designs differ upon implementation

virtues find balance in tested wisdom

grand illusions slip out

control refuses to be held accountable

reconstruction appreciates firm foundations

over-abundance of time

debate reasons not to decide

reality sits on strong shoulders

position firmly maintained

resting in the mold

who's in a hurry to break free?

playing board looks too crowded

no room to roll the die

substantial penalties for early withdrawal

the system constantly challenges you to obey it

—  —

orgasming alone

is like singing in an empty echoing cave

pleasure hasn't got a place to settle

melted ice-cream left to sit in the dish

thundering glimpses of starshine

sudden rainstorms preceeded by a few lightning strokes

passion splashes

— —

pleasure dances strong

technology stretches beyond tomorrow

mankind has ordered mechanical utopiazation,

complicating earth's orbit

space pollution poisons future generations

let's keep it clean

minute monkey tours a massive forest.
cathedral bells in chorus,
harmonizing centuries of religious control.
domination under guise of unification.
townfolk comment on traditions long ago established,
burned to the ground only to rise again.
Heaven's gates crash-shut.

My perspiration has first-strike capability,
maybe it can help achieve world peace.

coffeeshop privacy,

triple-buttered toast provides tonight's texture.

paced by afterthought explosions.

enlightment fuses wisdom and reality.


sorry serves no purpose.


priorities sharpen blunt edges,

defining the difference between having the condition

and being in it.

tomato juice never fully blends with ice

peanuts taste alive

vacuum sealed to exist forever

heartbeats in knuckles

swizzle sticks reveal need versus indulgence

tin-can expediency

imagination determines method of operation

this world's so intriguingly challenging
    I must bring a child into it
ultimate expansion of my soul
    another self to carry on my energy

reach out    dare to communicate with the world
it will take time to listen